In This Issue

II0069950

PIVOT MAGAZINE

Founder
Jason Miller

President
Juddene Villarin

Web Master
Joel Phillips

Designs
ReliableStaffSolutions.com

Copyright © 2025 PIVOT

ISBN: 978-1-957217-95-6

Contact
Jason Miller
Founder
1151 Eagle Drive #345
Loveland, CO 80537
jason@strategicadvisorboard.com

Shelby Jo Long
Editor-in-Chief
shelby@strategicadvisorboard.com
877-944-0944

From the Editor

What 2025 Really Taught Us

This issue is about the reset.

Not the flashy kind. The quiet, powerful one happening behind the scenes. Leaders are stepping back. Teams are rethinking how and where they work. Founders are rebuilding not for scale, but for sustainability. And a growing number of people are choosing craftsmanship over speed, clarity over chaos, and meaning over metrics.

You'll find all of that in this issue.

From the rise of third workplaces to the return of slow, high-trust business models, this edition captures the deeper shifts reshaping how we work, buy, build, and lead. It is not just about what is trending; it is about what is lasting.

As you move into a new chapter, let this issue be your blueprint for doing less, but doing it better.

Shelby Jo Long
Editor-in-Chief

A Different Kind of Growth

This year didn't just shift the market. It shifted the mindset.

The businesses gaining ground weren't chasing hype. They were optimizing for cashflow. They were listening to real buyer behavior. They were rebuilding on purpose, not panic.

In this issue, we take a closer look at what that kind of growth looks like. We explore why people are unplugging, why AI isn't the full story, and why the real competitive edge is still human.

This is not about going back to normal. It is about choosing a new normal that actually works.

So as you reflect on your own progress, ask yourself:

- What part of your business got clearer this year
- What distractions are worth leaving behind
- What version of leadership are you bringing into the next season

Let us build smarter. Let us lead slower. Let us make space for what matters most.

JUDDENE VILLARIN *J.V.*

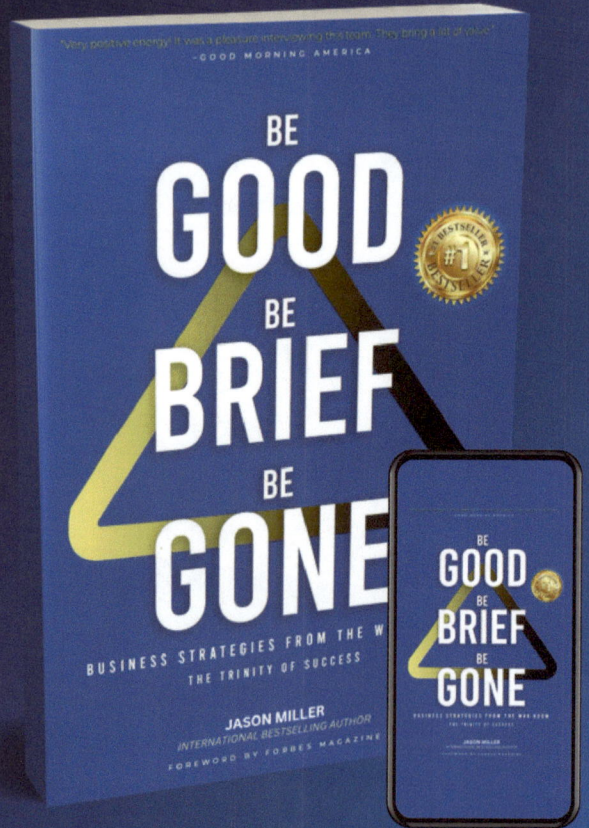
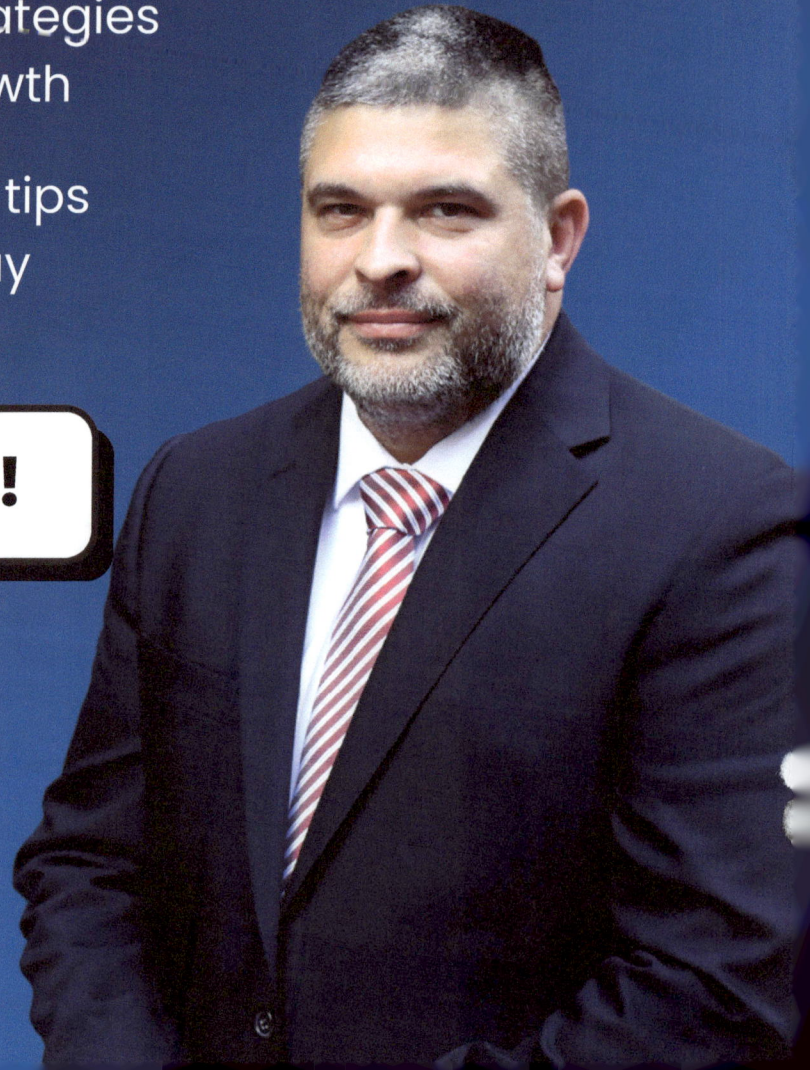

The Leadership Reset

What 2025 Taught Us About Power, People, and Performance

Leadership didn't lose power in 2025; it lost pretense. And in doing so, it became real again.

If 2020 cracked the old leadership model, 2025 exposed it.

The past year didn't reward the loudest leaders, the most visible executives, or the most charismatic personalities. It rewarded something quieter and far more difficult to fake: **competence paired with care.**

Across industries, the leaders who thrived weren't the ones clinging to hierarchy or charisma. They were the ones who adapted, listened, and redefined power in real time. Meanwhile, those who relied on control, fear, or performative authority found themselves bleeding talent, trust, and relevance.

2025 didn't create a leadership crisis.

It clarified one.

And what emerged was a reset; one that permanently altered how power, people, and performance intersect.

The Collapse of Command-and-Control

For decades, leadership meant decisiveness, dominance, and distance. Leaders made the calls. Teams executed. Information flowed downward. Power was positional.

That model worked when work was predictable and environments were stable.

But 2025 was anything but stable.

Supply chains fractured. AI disrupted workflows overnight. Labor expectations shifted. Markets oscillated between optimism and caution. Remote and global teams blurred the meaning of "oversight."

Command-and-control leadership couldn't keep up.

Leaders who insisted on control slowed decisions. Leaders who hoarded information created anxiety. Leaders who confused authority with intimidation lost their teams quietly; sometimes without resignations, sometimes with disengagement so deep it was indistinguishable from absence.

The old model didn't fail because people rebelled.

It failed because it couldn't scale to complexity.

Power Reframed: From Position to Permission

In 2025, power stopped coming from titles.

It came from **trust**.

The most effective leaders didn't assert authority; they earned followership. Their teams didn't comply; they committed.

This shift reframed power in three fundamental ways:

- From oversight to enablement

- From visibility to reliability

- From hierarchy to influence

Leaders gained power not by being seen, but by being useful.

They removed blockers. Clarified priorities. Made decisions faster. Took responsibility when things broke. And gave credit when things worked.

In an environment defined by uncertainty, people followed leaders who created clarity not fear.

The Hybrid Professional

For years, leadership had an aesthetic.

Visionary speeches. Inspirational posts.

Public vulnerability carefully calibrated for LinkedIn engagement. Leadership became a performance; something to be displayed rather than practiced.

In 2025, that performance collapsed.

Teams grew tired of leaders who talked about values but ignored workloads. Who spoke about empathy but dismissed burnout. Who celebrated "culture" while quietly optimizing people out of roles.

Employees stopped listening to what leaders said.

They watched what leaders did.

The gap between messaging and behavior became impossible to ignore. And in that gap, trust evaporated.

Authentic leadership wasn't

about being relatable.

It was about being consistent.

Performance Without Pressure

One of the biggest myths shattered in 2025 was the idea that pressure drives performance.

It doesn't.

It drives compliance.

High-performing teams didn't operate under constant urgency. They operated under clear expectations, psychological safety, and sustainable pace.

Leaders who understood this stopped managing emotions and started managing systems.

They:

- reduced unnecessary meetings

- clarified ownership

- simplified decision paths

- documented priorities

- respected focus time

- normalized rest

Performance improved not because people worked harder but because they worked cleaner.

The best leaders didn't push their teams.

They designed environments where pushing wasn't required.

Psychological Safety Became Operational

Once considered a "soft" concept, psychological safety became a measurable business variable in 2025.

Teams that felt safe:

- flagged risks earlier

- admitted mistakes faster

- innovated more freely

- collaborated more honestly

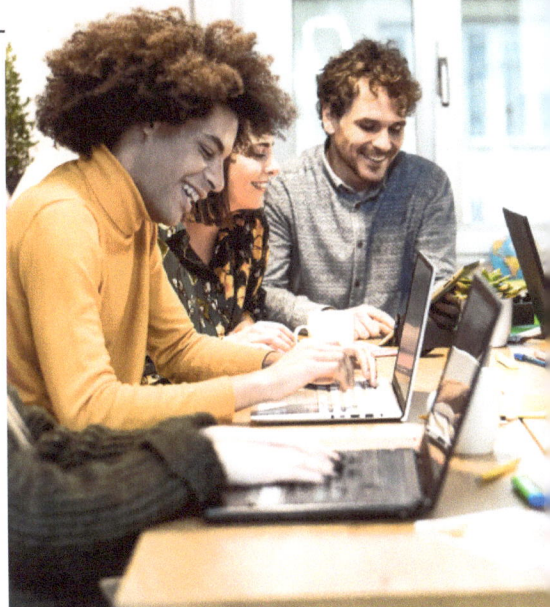

Teams that didn't?

They hid problems. Delayed bad news. Avoided accountability. And quietly failed.

Leaders learned that safety wasn't about comfort, it was about permission. Permission to speak. Permission to disagree. Permission to experiment.

The leaders who thrived didn't eliminate standards.

They eliminated fear.

The Leadership Skill That Outperformed All Others

If 2025 crowned a single defining leadership skill, it was this: clarity.

Not motivation. Not inspiration. Not charisma.

Clarity.

In volatile environments, clarity reduces cognitive load. It tells teams what matters, what doesn't, and where to focus.

The strongest leaders:

- communicated priorities repeatedly

- simplified goals relentlessly

- aligned decisions to strategy

- said no more often than yes

- made trade-offs visible

Their teams didn't feel micromanaged.

They felt anchored.

Clarity wasn't loud.

It was stabilizing.

The Rise of Distributed Authority

Leadership in 2025 wasn't centralized.

It was distributed.

The most effective organizations pushed decision-making closer to the work. Instead of routing everything through management layers, they empowered teams to act.

This required:

- clear decision frameworks

- defined ownership

- trust in judgment

- tolerance for imperfection

Leaders shifted from being decision-makers to decision designers.

They focused on building systems that allowed good decisions to happen without them.

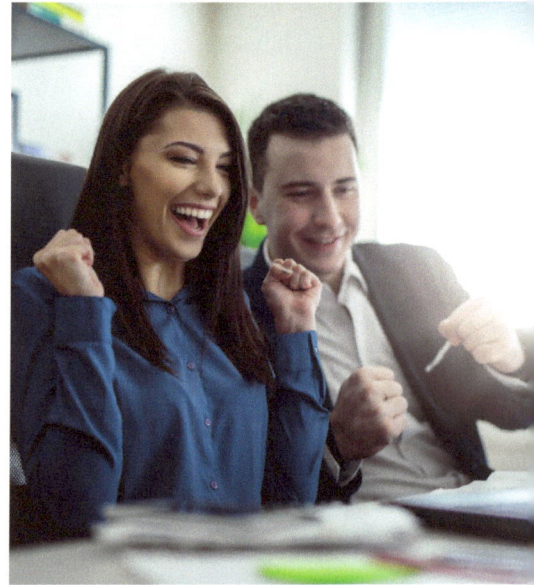

Control decreased.

Velocity increased.

Empathy Without Erosion

Empathy matured in 2025.

It stopped being emotional theater and became strategic awareness.

Effective leaders learned to hold two truths at once:

- people are human

- outcomes still matter

Empathy didn't mean lowering expectations.

It meant understanding constraints.

Leaders who mastered this balance:

- adjusted timelines without abandoning goals

- supported people without rescuing them

- listened without surrendering direction

This wasn't softness.

It was maturity.

Accountability Made a Comeback

After years of avoiding hard conversations in the name of "culture," accountability returned, cleaner and clearer.

The best leaders didn't weaponize accountability.

They normalized it.

Expectations were explicit. Feedback was direct. Consequences were fair and predictable.

This restored trust.

People don't resent accountability when it's consistent.

They resent ambiguity.

2025 reminded leaders that

kindness without standards breeds chaos and standards without kindness breed fear.

Real leadership requires both.

The Quiet Leaders Won

The most surprising outcome of 2025?

The quiet leaders outperformed the loud ones.

They weren't constantly visible. They weren't building personal brands. They weren't dominating conversations.

They were listening.

Designing.

Supporting.

Deciding.

Their teams were stable. Their execution steady. Their cultures resilient.

While others chased attention, these leaders built endurance.

And endurance won.

What 2025 Taught Us About Leadership

Leadership is no longer about:

- commanding attention

- controlling behavior

- performing authority

- projecting certainty

It's about:

- creating clarity

- earning trust

- designing systems

- distributing power

- sustaining performance

The reset wasn't ideological.

It was practical.

The leaders who adapted didn't do so because it was trendy.

They did it because the old way stopped working.

What This Means for Leaders Entering 2026

If you lead people, now or in the future, here's the blueprint 2025 left behind:

- Authority must be earned daily.

- Trust compounds faster than control.

- Clarity outperforms charisma.

- Systems matter more than speeches.

- Psychological safety is a performance multiplier.

- Accountability and empathy must coexist.

- Leadership is no longer positional; it's relational.

The era of leadership theater is over.

What replaces it is quieter, harder, and far more effective.

Leadership didn't lose power in 2025.

It lost pretense.

And in doing so, it became real again.

The Rise of the Third Workplace: Why Offices and Remote Aren't Enough Anymore

Work Didn't Disappear. It Escaped the Building.

For years, the debate felt binary.

Office or remote.

Cubicles or couches.

Commute or Zoom.

The future of work was framed as a choice between two extremes, and companies planted flags on either side like it was a culture war. But while leaders argued, workers quietly did something else.

They adapted.

In 2025, a new reality is impossible to ignore: the most productive, creative, and fulfilled professionals are no longer choosing between office and home. They're choosing **a third place**.

Not corporate headquarters.

Not the spare bedroom.

But something in between.

Welcome to the rise of the **Third Workplace**: a decentralized, flexible, human-centered evolution of where work actually happens.

The Limits of the Office

The office was never just about work. It was about control, visibility, and routine.

For decades, productivity was measured by presence. If you were seen at your desk, you were working. If you weren't, you were suspect. The office rewarded endurance, not output.

But by 2025, the cracks are undeniable.

Employees resent mandatory commutes that add nothing to performance. Open-plan offices drain focus. Meetings exist because people are together, not because they're needed. And the promise of "culture" often collapses into fluorescent lighting and bad coffee.

The data confirms it. Studies continue to show that most knowledge workers are productive for only a few focused hours per day. The rest is noise: interruptions, performative presence, unnecessary meetings.

The office didn't die.

It just stopped being the default.

The Limits of Remote Work

Remote work solved many problems but not all of them.

At first, working from home felt like freedom. No commute. No dress code. More autonomy. But over time, new issues emerged.

Homes weren't designed to be offices. Kitchen tables blurred into workstations. Workdays stretched into evenings. Isolation crept in. Collaboration became transactional. Creativity suffered without shared energy.

Remote work optimized efficiency, but often at the expense of connection.

The result? Burnout with better lighting.

By 2025, professionals began asking a new question. Not "Where do I work best?" but "Where do I feel most alive while working?"

That question sparked the third workplace.

What Is the Third Workplace?

The third workplace isn't one thing. It's a category.

It includes:

- coworking spaces

- hotel lobbies

- members-only clubs

- community studios

- creative hubs

- cafés designed for deep work

- local innovation centers

- flexible micro-offices

- hybrid collaboration spaces

These environments aren't home, and they're not corporate offices. They're intentional spaces designed for focus, connection, and autonomy.

The third workplace offers:

- structure without rigidity

- community without obligation

- professionalism without bureaucracy

It's where work meets life without consuming it.

Why Third Spaces Are Exploding Now

This isn't a trend. It's a correction.

Five forces are driving the rise of the third workplace:

1. Autonomy Became Non-Negotiable

Workers tasted control over their schedules and won't give it back. Third spaces preserve flexibility while restoring structure.

2. Isolation Became a Performance Issue

Loneliness isn't just emotional. It's operational. Third workplaces reintroduce human presence without forced interaction.

3. Creativity Needs Context

Ideas don't flourish in isolation or sterile offices. They thrive in

environments with energy, movement, and cross-pollination.

4. Work Is No Longer Location-Based

When your team spans time zones, the idea of a central office becomes obsolete. But people still crave "somewhere" to go.

5. Identity Shifted

People no longer want to be defined by their employer's

address. They want environments that reflect who they are, not who they work for.

The Psychology of Place

Where we work shapes how we think.

Environmental psychology shows that spaces influence cognition, motivation, and emotional regulation. Lighting, acoustics, layout, and even background noise affect performance.

Third workplaces succeed because they are designed intentionally, not inherited accidentally.

They offer:

- zones for deep focus

- spaces for informal collaboration

- visual variety that stimulates thinking

- social proximity without pressure

Unlike offices built for oversight or homes built for living, third spaces are built for thinking.

Coworking Grew Up

Early coworking spaces were chaotic; open tables, freelancers competing for outlets, noise masquerading as energy.

Today's third workplaces are different.

They're curated.

Segmented.

Purpose-built.

We're seeing:

- ndustry-specific coworking hubs

- executive-only memberships

- wellness-integrated workspaces

- creative studios with shared resources

- hybrid event-work environments

These spaces aren't just desks, they're ecosystems.

They provide:

- community programming

- mentorship access

- learning events

- collaboration opportunities

The third workplace isn't about renting space.

It's about belonging to a professional environment without surrendering independence.

The Corporate Pivot No One Is Talking About

Behind the scenes, companies

are quietly adjusting.

Instead of renewing massive office leases, many organizations are:

- subsidizing coworking memberships

- offering flexible workspace stipends

- partnering with local third spaces

- creating "hub-and-spoke" models

- downsizing HQs into collaboration centers

This allows companies to reduce overhead while giving employees choice.

It's a silent pivot but a strategic one.

RSS>
Reliable Staff Solutions

STAFF SPOTLIGHT

Designing with Dedication:
Marie Justine Galido

Versatility, Family, and the Art of Going the Extra Mile

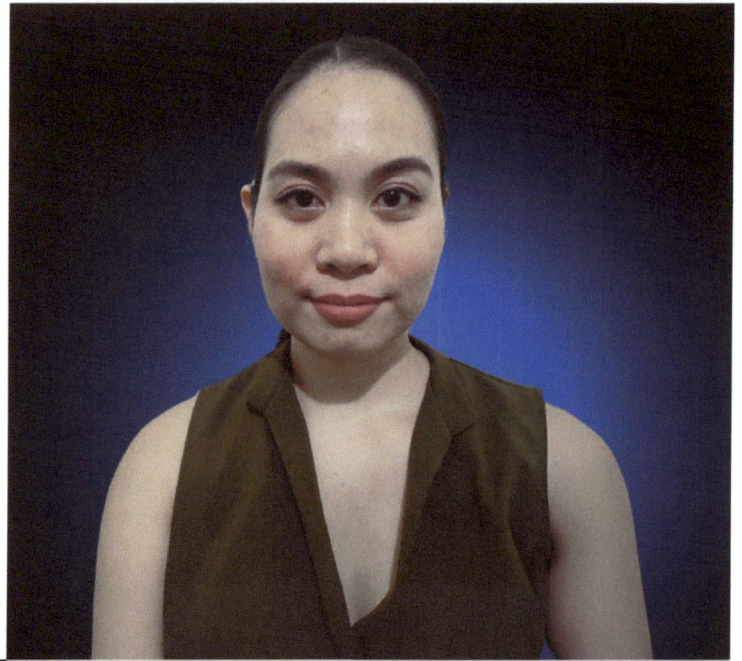

"Working at RSS has taught me the importance of responsibility and the value of delivering outstanding work"

When did you join the RSS team, and what brought you here?

I've been working with Juddene since before RSS officially existed, and when Jason & Juddene launched the company, they included me, which I'm truly grateful for.

What's your favorite part of working at RSS?

I'm thankful that my personal time is respected. Every client I've worked with has maintained a positive relationship, which makes the work fulfilling.

How has your role evolved since you started?

Taking on multiple tasks has made me more versatile. I continue learning new skills to grow and improve in every assignment.

Describe your typical workday or work-from-home setup

I work during the day while caring for my toddler, then handle any urgent tasks in the evening. It's a busy rhythm, but it works and keeps me productive.

If you could describe RSS in three words, what would they be?

Harmony, Family, Mastery

STAFF STATS

🎧 **Work Anthem:** Relaxing OPM playlist

🍪 **Favorite Snack:** Classic Nescafé and sweet treats

💡 **Fun Fact:** Loves road trips & board games with friends despite busy schedules

"

Being reliable, to me, means prioritizing consistency in how I serve my clients and manage my responsibilities.

The smartest leaders understand that forcing people back into offices won't rebuild culture. Designing better places to work will.

The Third Workplace and Leadership

Leadership changes when work leaves the building.

You can't manage by presence when your team works everywhere. You have to manage by outcomes, trust, and clarity.

Third workplaces reward leaders who:

- communicate clearly
- set expectations explicitly
- empower autonomy
- respect focus
- measure results, not visibility

This shift exposes weak leadership fast.

Managers who relied on oversight struggle.

Leaders who build trust thrive.

The third workplace doesn't just change where work happens. It changes how leadership works.

Creativity Loves Collision

One of the most overlooked benefits of third workplaces is cross-disciplinary collision.

In traditional offices, everyone works for the same company. In remote settings, you interact almost exclusively with your own team.

In third workplaces, you sit next to:

- founders
- designers
- developers
- writers
- strategists
- consultants
- investors

Ideas cross-pollinate organically. Conversations spark unexpected insight. Problems get solved by people outside your industry.

This kind of creative friction is nearly impossible to manufacture in corporate settings and nearly absent in remote isolation.

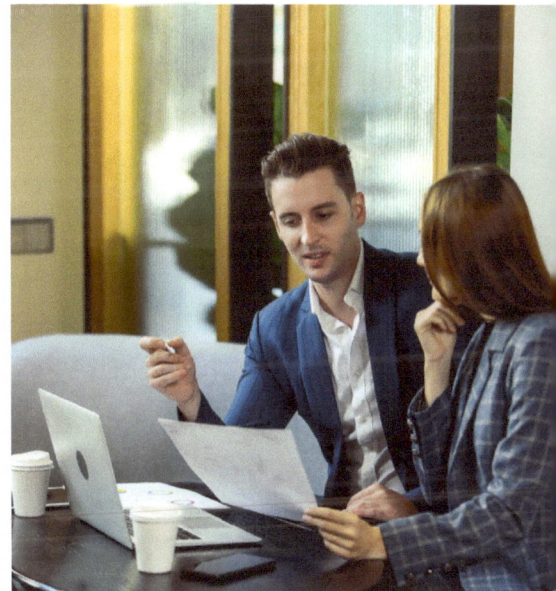

Third spaces bring back serendipity.

The Economic Impact of Third Workplaces

This shift isn't just cultural, it's

These workers aren't anti-office or anti-remote.

They're pro-choice.

The Future Isn't Hybrid. It's Modular.

The biggest mistake companies make is calling this "hybrid work."

Hybrid implies compromise: half office, half remote.

The future isn't compromise.

It's modularity.

People will choose:

- when to work alone

- when to collaborate

- where to focus

economic.

Local third workplaces:

- revive downtown areas

- support small businesses

- reduce traffic congestion

- decentralize economic opportunity

- create micro-communities of innovation

Instead of wealth and opportunity clustering in major cities, talent disperses and takes spending power with it.

The third workplace is quietly reshaping urban economies.

Who Thrives Most in the Third Workplace?

While almost anyone can benefit, certain groups are leading the shift:

- Founders and entrepreneurs who need focus and energy without corporate drag

- Remote professionals craving structure and social presence

- Creatives who think better in dynamic environments

- Consultants and fractional leaders who operate across companies

- where to connect

And they'll assemble their workweek like a playlist not a prescription.

The third workplace is a module. Not a mandate

Designing Work Around Humans Again

For too long, humans adapted to systems.

Now systems must adapt to humans.

The rise of the third workplace signals a deeper shift: work is being redesigned around how people actually function, not how organizations prefer to manage.

This is a return to:

- trust over surveillance
- autonomy over control
- design over default

Work didn't become flexible because of technology.

It became flexible because people demanded dignity.

What This Means for Entrepreneurs and Leaders

If you're building a business in 2026, here's the takeaway:

- Stop forcing binary choices.
- Give people options, not orders.
- Invest in environments, not buildings.
- Design systems that assume trust.
- Let people choose where they do their best work.

The third workplace isn't a perk.

It's a performance advantage.

Because when people feel supported by their environment, they don't just work better; They stay longer, think deeper, and contribute more fully.

The Quiet Revolution

There will be no headline announcing the death of the office or the end of remote work.

Instead, there will be something subtler.

Cafés filled with focused professionals at noon.

Coworking spaces humming with collaboration.

Hotel lobbies doubling as boardrooms.

Community studios hosting strategy sessions.

Work will continue, just not where we expected.

The third workplace isn't coming. It's already here.

And the companies that recognize it now won't just attract talent.

They'll unlock the next evolution of how work actually works.

The Return of Craftsmanship: Why Slow Work Is Becoming a Competitive Advantage

Speed Built the Internet. Craft Will Save It.

For the last two decades, speed was the ultimate advantage.

Move fast. Ship faster. Scale first. Fix later.

Entire industries were built on velocity. Products launched half-finished. Companies prioritized growth over depth. Content flooded feeds before ideas had time to mature. Being first mattered more than being right.

And for a while, it worked.

But by the end of 2025, something undeniable happened: **speed stopped impressing people.**

Customers grew wary of rushed products. Employees burned out from endless urgency. Leaders realized that constant acceleration created fragility, not strength. And in a marketplace drowning in sameness, fast became forgettable.

In its place, something unexpected returned.

Craftsmanship.

The Exhaustion of Acceleration

The modern economy ran on urgency for too long.

Businesses optimized for output at the expense of quality. Teams sprinted endlessly without recovery. "Done" mattered more than "done well." The cost was hidden at first, then painfully obvious.

Rushed decisions created technical debt.

Rushed messaging eroded trust.

Rushed growth collapsed under its own weight.

Consumers began to notice. They encountered products that felt flimsy, content that felt hollow, and brands that felt interchangeable.

The faster everything moved, the less meaningful it felt.

innovation.

Now it signals shortcuts.

And shortcuts don't build loyalty.

What Craftsmanship Actually Means Now

Craftsmanship isn't nostalgia.

It isn't slowness for slowness' sake.

And it isn't resistance to technology.

Modern craftsmanship is **intentional excellence.**

It's the discipline of doing fewer things better.

The commitment to depth over volume.

The willingness to say no to speed when it compromises integrity.

Craftsmanship shows up as:

- products designed to last

- services delivered with care

- writing that sounds human, not optimized

- businesses that choose sustainability over spectacle

It's not about being slow.

It's about being deliberate.

And in 2025, deliberateness became rare which made it valuable.

Why Fast Became Fragile

Speed amplifies weakness.

When systems are rushed, cracks spread faster. When teams are overloaded, mistakes compound. When growth outpaces infrastructure, collapse becomes inevitable.

We've seen it repeatedly:

- Startups that scaled before product-market fit

- Platforms that grew users faster than trust

- Brands that chased virality instead of reliability

Fast growth without strong foundations creates brittle organizations.

Craftsmanship, on the other hand, builds resilience. It favors durability over drama.

The most stable companies of 2025 weren't the fastest movers.

They were the most disciplined builders.

The Trust Economy Rewards Craft

Trust is the new currency.

And trust isn't built quickly.

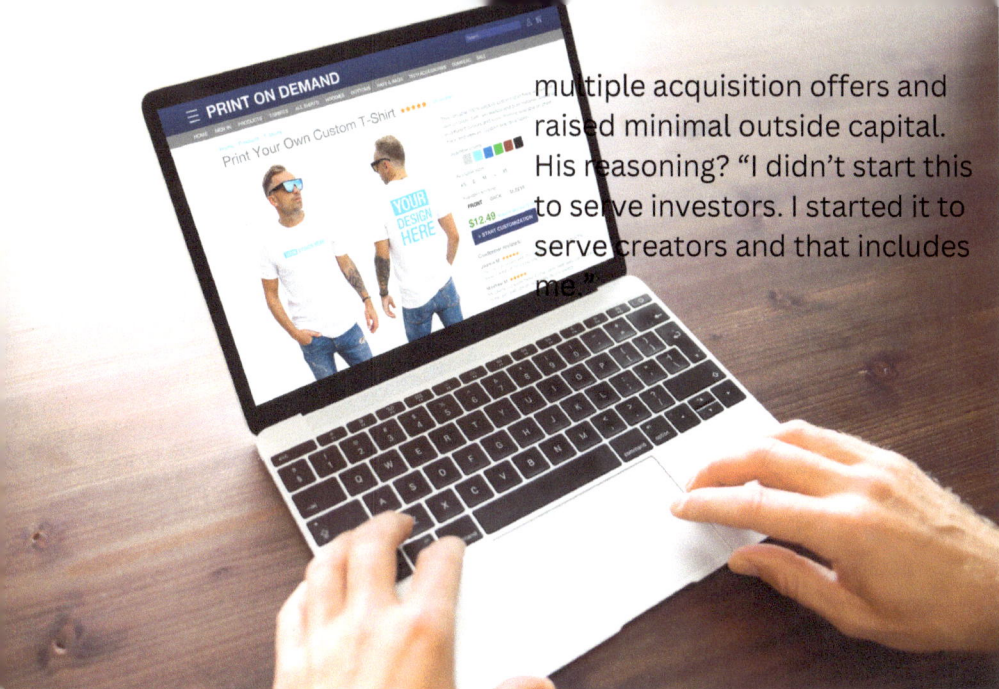

multiple acquisition offers and raised minimal outside capital. His reasoning? "I didn't start this to serve investors. I started it to serve creators and that includes me."

- restraint in automation

The companies winning with AI aren't using it to replace craft. They're using it to support craft.

Speed without discernment floods the market.

Craft with leverage rises above it.

Slow Work Is Not Lazy Work

One of the biggest misconceptions about craftsmanship is that it's inefficient.

It's not.

Slow work eliminates rework.

It reduces errors, clarifies decisions, and improves outcomes.

Customers don't trust what looks rushed. They trust what feels considered. They trust brands that show restraint, care, and consistency.

That's why handcrafted brands are resurging across industries:

- small-batch manufacturing

- bespoke services

- long-form content

- premium consulting

- artisan digital products

These businesses don't compete on volume.

They compete on credibility.

And credibility compounds.

In a marketplace full of shortcuts, craftsmanship becomes a signal: **someone cared enough to do this right.**

Craftsmanship in the Age of AI

Ironically, AI accelerated the return of craftsmanship.

When machines made it easy to produce content, designs, and code at scale, human-made work stood out instantly. People began to value the imperfections that signal thought, judgment, and care.

AI can generate fast. Humans refine slow.

The difference is obvious.

Craftsmanship in the AI era looks like:

- human-edited AI output

- thoughtful prompts shaped by expertise

- intentional pacing

- clear voice and point of view

When teams rush, they revisit decisions constantly. When they work deliberately, they move forward cleanly.

Craftsmanship optimizes for total cost, not just immediate speed.

The companies embracing this approach in 2025 saw:

- fewer mistakes

- better margins

- higher retention

- stronger brand loyalty

- more pride in work

Slow work isn't about moving less.

It's about moving with intention.

The Rise of the Specialist Creator

In content, craftsmanship is reshaping who gets attention.

Mass posting no longer wins. Depth does.

Creators who publish less, but say more, are building durable audiences. Long-form essays, thoughtful analysis, and well-researched insights outperform daily noise.

Audiences are tired of endless output. They're hungry for substance.

The rise of:

- newsletters over feeds

- podcasts over clips

- essays over threads

isn't accidental. It's a reaction to saturation.

Crafted ideas cut through where fast content blends in.

Craft as a Leadership Signal

Leaders are rediscovering craftsmanship, too.

Not in optics but in decision-making.

The strongest leaders of 2025:

- slowed decisions when stakes were high

- resisted pressure to react publicly

- prioritized long-term outcomes over short-term wins

- built systems carefully instead of patching constantly

They didn't confuse urgency with importance.

Craftsmanship in leadership means:

- thoughtful communication
- consistent standards
- disciplined execution
- intentional culture design

It's quieter.

But it's far more effective.

Why Craftsmanship Scales Better Than Speed

Speed looks scalable because it's repeatable.

Craftsmanship scales because it's respected.

People copy what works. They don't copy what's disposable.

Craft builds:

- word-of-mouth

- reputation
- loyalty
- pricing power

Fast growth attracts attention. Craft attracts advocates.

That distinction matters when markets tighten.

The Return of Pride in Work

Perhaps the most profound shift of all: people want to feel proud of what they produce again.

Years of hustle culture trained workers to prioritize output over ownership. Burnout followed. Disengagement followed. Quiet quitting followed.

Craftsmanship restores meaning.

When people are allowed to do work well, not just quickly, they reconnect with purpose. Pride replaces pressure. Mastery replaces exhaustion.

This isn't sentimental.

It's operational.

Teams that care produce better results.

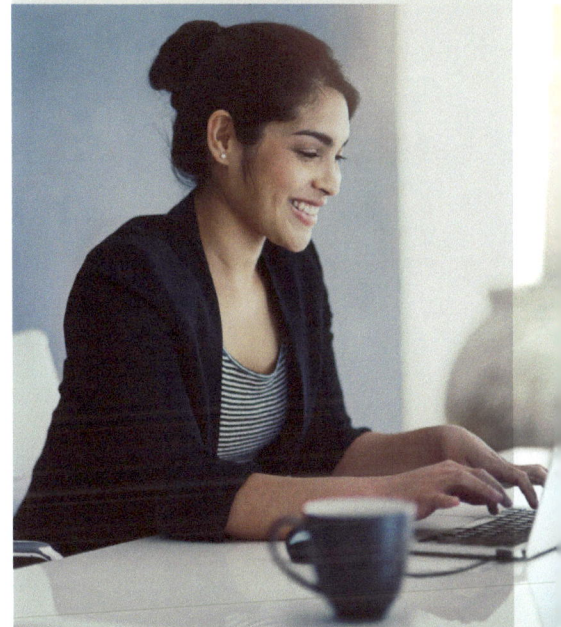

Industries Where Craft Is Winning

Across sectors, the pattern is clear:

- **Software**: Fewer features, better UX
- **E-commerce**: Fewer SKUs, higher quality
- **Consulting**: Fewer clients, deeper engagement
- **Media**: Fewer posts, stronger perspective
- **Manufacturing**: Smaller runs, better materials

The businesses leaning into craft aren't shrinking. They're refining. And refinement scales differently but more sustainably.

Craftsmanship as Strategy

Craft isn't a creative choice. It's a strategic one.

It allows businesses to:

- differentiate without shouting

- command premium pricing

- reduce churn

- build defensible reputations

- attract aligned talent

In competitive markets, craftsmanship becomes the moat.

It's hard to replicate care, to fake intention, and to copy pride.

That difficulty is the advantage.

What This Means for Entrepreneurs

If you're building something going into 2026, the question isn't "How fast can I grow?"

It's:

- How well is this built?

- Will this last?

- Does this reflect what I stand for?

- Would I be proud to put my name on this in five years?

Craftsmanship requires patience but patience pays.

Not immediately but enduringly.

The Cultural Correction

The return of craftsmanship isn't regression. It's a correction.

A recalibration after years of excess speed. A reminder that quality still matters. A recognition that humans crave meaning, not momentum.

Speed built the modern economy. Craft will stabilize it.

And in a world moving faster than ever, the businesses willing to slow down, just enough to do things right, will be the ones still standing when others burn out.

The Competitive Advantage No One Can Copy

Anyone can move fast. Few are willing to care deeply.

Craftsmanship requires:

- restraint

- discipline

- patience

- pride

Those qualities can't be automated.

They can't be rushed.

And they can't be outsourced. That's why craftsmanship is returning, not as a trend, but as a competitive necessity.

Because when everything is fast, the work that lasts wins.

The Quiet Pivot: How Businesses Are Rebuilding Behind the Scenes While the Market Sleeps

The Loud Ones Are Talking. The Smart Ones Are Rebuilding.

Not every pivot comes with a press release.

Not every transformation announces itself on social media. And not every winning strategy is visible in real time.

In 2025, while headlines focused on market volatility, AI disruption, and economic uncertainty, a quieter story unfolded beneath the surface. Businesses didn't panic. They paused. They observed. And then, out of public view, they rebuilt.

No rebrands.

No hype cycles.

No dramatic announcements.

Just careful, deliberate change.

Welcome to the era of the quiet pivot, where the smartest companies stop eacting to noise and start redesigning fundamentals while everyone else is distracted.

When Loud Becomes Risky

The last decade trained companies to move publicly. Launch fast. Announce big. Share every update. Perform momentum.

But by 2025, visibility itself became a liability. Markets punished overconfidence.

Customers scrutinized claims more closely. Competitors copied ideas in days. And public pivots invited public judgment before strategies had time to mature.

So leaders changed tactics.

They stopped narrating every move, testing strategies in public, and confusing attention with progress.

Instead, they went quiet and got

DOING GOOD IS GOOD BUSINESS

SHARING THE CREDIT

serious.

What a Quiet Pivot Actually Is

A quiet pivot isn't inaction. It's intentional reconstruction.

It's when companies:

- rework business models without rebranding

- restructure teams without public drama

- rebuild operations without announcing "transformation"

- test new offers quietly with small segments

- reduce risk before scaling again

It's strategic humility.

Rather than chasing validation, these companies focus on alignment. Rather than reacting to trends, they redesign foundations.

Quiet pivots aren't slow. They're discreet.

Why 2025 Made Silence Strategic

Three forces made quiet pivots not just smart but necessary.

1. Public Markets Punished Uncertainty

Investors grew wary of companies that pivoted loudly. Big announcements without proven traction triggered skepticism.

Silence bought time.

2. Customers Became Hyper-Skeptical

Audiences learned to distrust big promises. Overexposed pivots looked desperate.

Quiet change rebuilt trust before visibility returned.

3. Competition Accelerated

Ideas spread instantly. Loud experimentation invited copycats.

Stealth protected advantage.

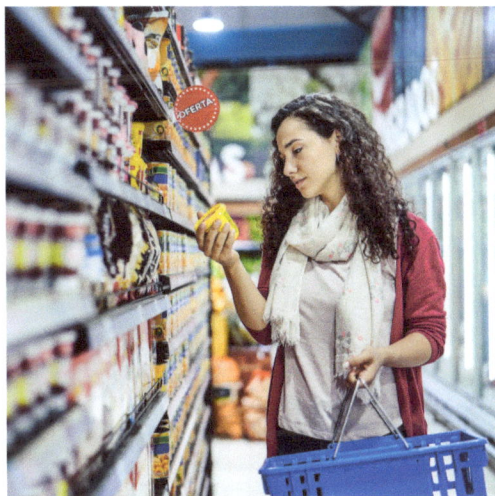

The smartest leaders recognized this shift early and adjusted accordingly.

The Hidden Work Nobody Brags About

Quiet pivots focus on unglamorous work, the kind that never trends online but determines long-term survival.

That includes:

- renegotiating vendor contracts

- simplifying product lines

- fixing broken onboarding

- cleaning up technical debt

- improving unit economics

- tightening messaging

- clarifying ICPs

- rebuilding SOPs

- retraining teams

- resetting incentives

This isn't flashy work but it's decisive.

While others chase optics, quiet pivoters rebuild substance.

The Strategic Power of Boring Decisions

The quiet pivot favors boring decisions because boring decisions compound.

- Cutting underperforming SKUs.

- Exiting low-margin clients.

- Pausing expansion.

- Delaying launches.

- Reducing complexity

These moves don't make headlines. They make companies stronger.

In 2025, founders learned that resilience isn't built through

gestures; it's built through disciplined subtraction.

Less noise, more margin, and clearer focus.

Quiet Pivots Inside Organizations

Internally, the quiet pivot looks like clarity without chaos.

Instead of dramatic restructures, leaders:

- redefined roles gradually

- reallocated responsibilities quietly

- reduced meetings methodically

- introduced new workflows incrementally

- reset expectations clearly

This prevented shock and preserved morale.

Employees weren't blindsided. They were brought along.

Quiet pivots respect people while correcting systems.

The Product Quiet Pivot

Some of the most impactful pivots in 2025 happened at the product level and went completely unnoticed externally.

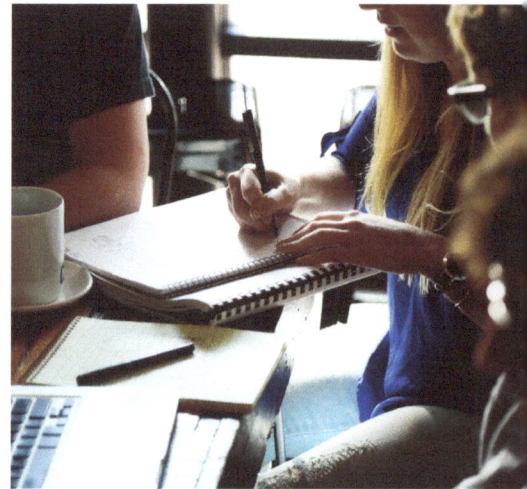

Companies:

- narrowed feature sets

- focused on core use cases

- killed complexity

- improved reliability

- rebuilt UX from scratch

- tested pricing quietly

No announcements. Just better products.

When they re-emerged publicly, customers didn't hear about a pivot; they felt it.

That's the difference.

The Revenue Quiet Pivot

Revenue strategies quietly shifted, too.

Instead of chasing volume, companies focused on:

- profitability over growth

- retention over acquisition

- lifetime value over reach

- fewer customers with higher

alignment

This led to:

- pricing changes rolled out selectively

- contract structures simplified

- upsell paths clarified

- customer segments refined

The loud playbook said "grow at all costs."

The quiet pivot said "build something that lasts."

Marketing Went Quiet And Smarter

Marketing teams were some of the first to pivot quietly.

They:

- reduced posting frequency

- stopped chasing virality

- invested in owned channels

- built content libraries

- improved conversion paths

- refined messaging deeply

Instead of shouting louder, they spoke more clearly.

Traffic dipped initially. Conversions improved steadily.

Quiet marketing traded attention for trust.

Quiet Pivots and Leadership Maturity

The quiet pivot is a leadership maturity test.

It requires:

- confidence without applause

- patience without reassurance

- decision-making without external validation

- tolerance for temporary invisibility

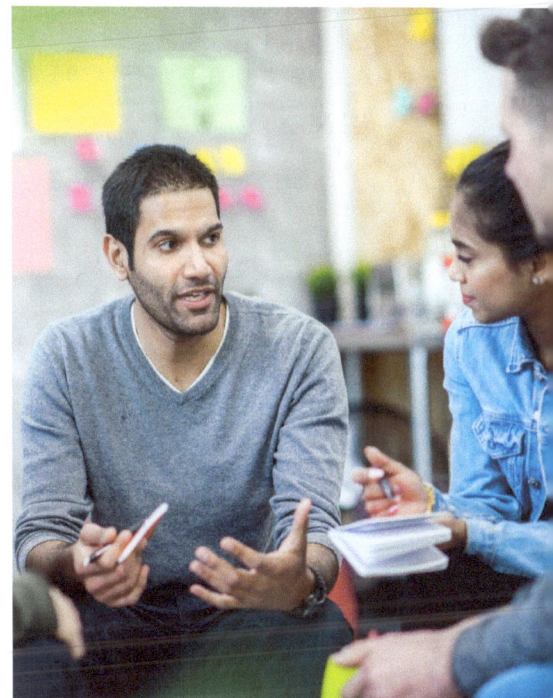

Not all leaders can handle that. Some need attention to feel progress.

Others understand that progress often happens in silence.

2025 rewarded the second group.

Case Pattern: Who Quiet Pivots Best

Across industries, the same types of leaders executed quiet pivots successfully:

- founder-led companies with long-term vision

- bootstrapped or lightly funded businesses

- operators with strong financial literacy

- leaders comfortable saying no

- teams aligned on purpose over hype

These organizations didn't need to perform success.

They were building it.

The Psychological Advantage of Silence

Silence creates space.

It allows leaders to:

- think clearly

- analyze deeply

- test privately

- fail safely

- adjust intelligently

Noise compresses decision-making. Silence expands it.

Quiet pivots restore strategic depth.

Why Loud Pivots Usually Fail

Loud pivots often fail for predictable reasons:

- expectations outpace execution

- teams feel rushed

- strategies are underdeveloped

- customers scrutinize too early

- pressure forces premature scaling

Visibility becomes a constraint instead of an asset.

Quiet pivots avoid this trap entirely.

The Return of Strategic Patience

Perhaps the most radical shift of 2025 was the return of patience as a business virtue.

Not complacency.

Not hesitation.

Strategic patience.

The understanding that:

- timing matters

- foundations matter

- alignment matters

The quiet pivot is patience in motion.

What This Means for Entrepreneurs

If you're building going into 2026, the lesson is simple:

You don't owe the market a narrative while you're rebuilding.

You owe yourself clarity.

Your team stability.

Your customers value.

Not every move needs applause.

Some of the most important work happens when nobody is watching.

When to Pivot Quietly and When Not To

Quiet pivots work best when:

- fundamentals are broken

- strategy needs rethinking

- execution needs tightening

- confidence needs rebuilding

Loud pivots still matter when:

- entering new markets

- repositioning brands

- signaling major shifts

The wisdom is knowing the difference.

The Quiet Pivot Isn't Passive

It's disciplined, focused, and intentional.

It's choosing progress over

performance.

While others announce change, quiet pivoters create it.

The Payoff Comes Later

The reward for quiet pivots doesn't arrive immediately.

It arrives when:

- margins stabilize

- teams execute smoothly

- customers notice improvements

- competitors fall behind

- growth returns organically

By the time the market realizes what happened, it's already too late to catch up.

The Quiet Pivot Isn't Passive

The companies that dominate 2026 won't be the loudest.

They'll be the ones who:

- rebuilt while others reacted

- refined while others rushed

- strengthened while others shouted

The quiet pivot isn't a trend. It's a strategy for uncertain times.

And right now, uncertainty is the only constant.

Final Thought

You don't need attention to rebuild.

You need discipline.

You don't need applause to pivot.

You need clarity.

And sometimes, the smartest move a business can make is to go quiet, long enough to get it right.

Cashflow Over Chaos: Why Lean, "Boring" Businesses Are Outperforming Startups

Flash Gets Funded. Cashflow Survives.

For years, entrepreneurship was sold as spectacle.

Pitch decks. Demo days. Unicorn dreams. Explosive growth charts climbing straight up and to the right.

If your business wasn't "scalable," it wasn't serious.

If it wasn't "disruptive," it wasn't interesting.

If it wasn't burning capital fast, it wasn't ambitious enough.

Then reality caught up.

By the end of 2025, a quiet truth became impossible to ignore: while flashy startups struggled to justify valuations and burn rates, a different class of business was quietly winning.

They weren't exciting.

They weren't trending on social media.

They weren't chasing press.

They were profitable.

Welcome to the return of the **lean, boring business** and why cashflow has become the most powerful competitive advantage in an uncertain economy.

The Collapse of the Growth-at-All-Costs Myth

The growth-at-all-costs era relied on three assumptions:

1. Capital would always be cheap

2. Customers would always

tolerate inefficiency

3. Exit opportunities would always exist

By 2025, all three collapsed.

Interest rates rose. Investors demanded proof, not promises. Customers became more selective. And exits became rarer, slower, and more scrutinized.

Suddenly, growth without profit wasn't bold; it was reckless.

Companies that once bragged about user counts now scrambled to explain margins. Founders who optimized for valuation had to relearn how to run businesses.

The era of financial theater ended and the era of financial discipline began.

What "Boring" Actually Means

Boring doesn't mean stagnant.

It means predictable.

Boring businesses are:

- service-based
- repeatable
- operationally efficient
- margin-aware
- customer-centric
- cashflow positive

They sell unsexy things:

- logistics
- healthcare services
- trades
- accounting
- staffing
- software tools with narrow use cases
- niche B2B solutions

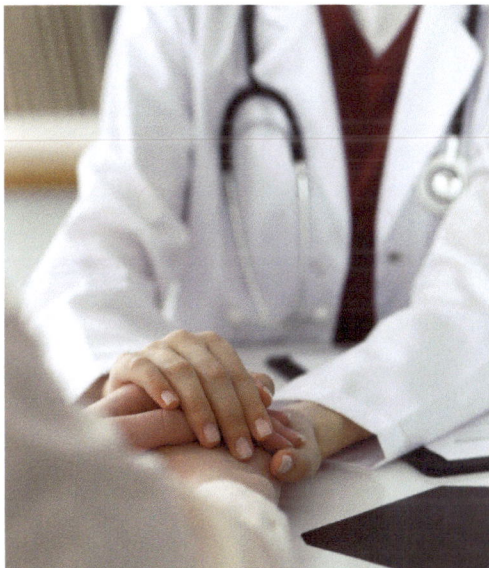

They don't chase virality.

They chase reliability.

And reliability pays consistently.

Cashflow Is Control

Cashflow does something venture capital never can: it gives you options.

Businesses with steady cashflow can:

- survive downturns
- invest selectively
- hire deliberately
- pivot without panic
- say no to bad deals
- play the long game

Businesses without it live quarter to quarter, constantly negotiating their own survival.

In 2025, founders rediscovered a hard truth: Cashflow isn't boring. It's freedom.

Why Lean Businesses Adapt Faster

Lean companies don't have layers of approval. They don't have bloated overhead.

They don't have to justify burn to investors.

They can change course quickly because they aren't anchored by complexity.

When costs rise, they adjust pricing.

When demand shifts, they shift focus.

When technology changes, they adapt workflows.

They don't need consensus from a boardroom full of people who aren't in the trenches.

Lean businesses don't move slower than startups.

They move cleaner.

The Rise of the Anti-Unicorn Founder

A new founder archetype is emerging.

They don't chase unicorn status. They chase durability.

They care about:

- profit per employee
- customer lifetime value
- churn rates
- operational efficiency
- time freedom
- personal sanity

They aren't interested in scaling teams unnecessarily.

They're interested in scaling systems.

This founder doesn't pitch. They build.

And they sleep better.

Why Customers Prefer Boring

Customers don't want disruption. They want dependability.

They want:

- services that work
- products that last

- support that responds

- pricing that makes sense

The novelty of flashy brands fades quickly. The trust built by consistent delivery doesn't.

In 2025, customers gravitated toward businesses that felt stable, not experimental.

Boring businesses don't overpromise. They deliver.

That reliability creates loyalty. Loyalty creates recurring revenue.

Recurring revenue creates resilience.

Operational Excellence Beat Vision

Vision still matters but it's no longer enough.

The companies outperforming in 2025 were operationally sound:

- clean books

- clear processes

- documented systems

- defined roles

- controlled costs

They didn't rely on heroics. They relied on repeatability.

Operational excellence isn't inspiring but it's unstoppable.

Bootstrapping's Quiet Comeback

Bootstrapping used to be framed as a limitation. Now it's a strategy.

Bootstrapped companies:

- stay close to customers

- price rationally

- grow intentionally

- avoid unnecessary complexity

Without investor pressure, founders make decisions based on sustainability not optics.

Bootstrapping forces clarity. Clarity produces discipline. Discipline produces profit.

The Margin Mindset

One of the biggest shifts in 2025 was the return of margin thinking.

Instead of asking: "How fast can we grow?"

Founders asked: "How profitable is each decision?"

This led to:

- fewer SKUs

- fewer clients

- higher-quality customers

- stronger positioning

- cleaner execution

Margins became strategy not accounting.

Why Venture-Backed and Lean Can't Be Compared Anymore

For years, lean businesses were compared to startups as if they were competing in the same race.

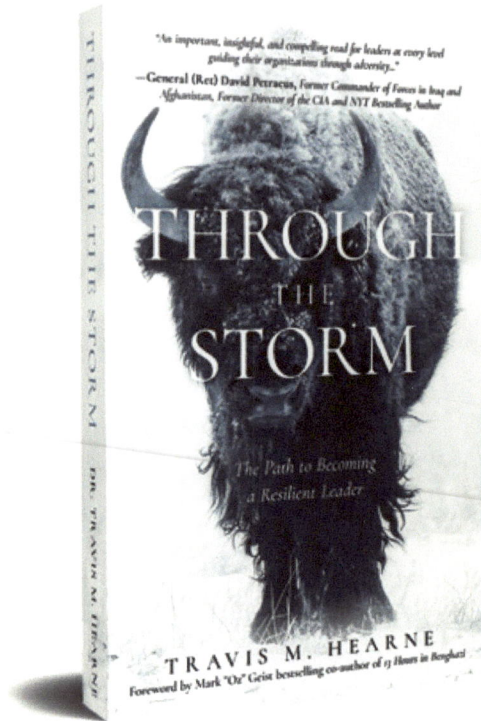

They aren't.

Venture-backed startups optimize for scale and exit. Lean businesses optimize for longevity and cashflow.

Different goals.

Different rules.

Different outcomes.

In a stable market, both can succeed.

In a volatile one, cashflow wins.

The Psychological Advantage of Profitability

Profitability changes how founders think.

They stop chasing validation.
They stop fearing runway.
They stop reacting emotionally.

They think clearly.

Profit removes desperation from decision-making.

And desperation is expensive.

Quiet Empires Are Everywhere

Look closely and you'll find them:

- regional service companies with decades-long histories

- family-owned businesses modernizing operations

- B2B firms with small teams and massive margins

- digital service providers with loyal niche clients

They don't headline TechCrunch.
They don't trend on LinkedIn.

But they endure.

The Cultural Shift Around Success

The definition of success is changing.

Success is no longer:

- raising a big round

- hiring hundreds

- chasing a massive exit

Success is:

- predictable revenue

- manageable growth

- personal freedom

- strong margins

- optionality

Founders are optimizing for lives not legends.

Why "Boring" Is the New Strategic Edge

Boring businesses:

- weather storms

- outlast trends

- attract serious customers

- retain great employees

- compound steadily

They don't rely on hype cycles.
They rely on fundamentals.

And fundamentals don't go out of style.

What This Means for Entrepreneurs

If you're building toward 2026, ask yourself:

- Does this business generate real cash?

- Can it survive without external funding?

- Are margins healthy?

- Is growth sustainable?

- Would this still work in a downturn?

If the answer is yes, you're already ahead.

The Future Belongs to the Boring

Innovation will continue. Startups will still exist. Disruption will still happen.

But the backbone of the economy, the businesses that quietly employ millions and create real value, will be lean, disciplined, and cashflow-driven.

Boring businesses aren't behind the times.

They're built for them.

Final Thought

Hype fades quickly, but cashflow compounds quietly over time.

In an economy that values endurance over excitement, the boldest move isn't chasing attention; it's building something intentionally boring, stable, and profitable.

Founders who prioritize durability over flash create businesses that survive cycles, weather downturns, and reward patience instead of noise.

Buyer Behavior Reinvented: The New Psychology of How People Make Decisions

People Don't Buy Faster Anymore. They Buy Smarter.

For years, marketing relied on speed.

Urgency. Scarcity. Countdown timers. Limited offers. Buy now or miss out.

It worked until it didn't.

By the end of 2025, something fundamental shifted in how people make decisions. Buyers slowed down. They questioned more. They compared longer. They resisted pressure. And most importantly, they stopped responding to the psychological triggers that once drove conversion rates sky-high.

This wasn't hesitation. It was discernment.

The modern buyer isn't impulsive; they're informed. They aren't indecisive; they're protective. In an economy shaped by volatility, misinformation, and overload, decision-making evolved into a survival skill.

Welcome to the new psychology of buying where trust, clarity, and alignment matter more than persuasion ever did.

The End of the Impulse Economy

Impulse buying thrived in an environment of excess. Cheap money. Predictable growth. Endless novelty. When tomorrow felt secure, spending today felt harmless.

That environment is gone.

Economic uncertainty trained consumers to pause. Layoffs, inflation, and constant disruption reshaped financial instincts. People learned to ask harder questions before committing money, time, or loyalty.

Impulse didn't disappear.

It matured.

Buyers became intentional.

They didn't stop spending. They stopped rushing.

Decision Fatigue Changed Everything

The average consumer is bombarded with thousands of marketing messages daily. Choices multiplied. Options expanded. Customization became infinite.

And the brain hit its limit.

Decision fatigue is now one of the strongest forces shaping buyer behavior. When overwhelmed, people don't choose the "best" option; they choose the safest one. Or they choose nothing at all.

This is why brands that simplify decision-making outperform

those that overwhelm.

More features don't convert. Clear positioning does.

In 2025, the most effective brands weren't louder. They were clearer.

Trust Replaced Persuasion

Traditional marketing focused on convincing.

Modern buying focuses on believing.

People no longer ask, "Do I want this?"

They ask, "Do I trust this?"

Trust became the gatekeeper of conversion.

And trust isn't built through clever copy. It's built through:

- consistency

- transparency

- proof

- reputation

- experience

Buyers don't want to be persuaded. They want to feel safe making the decision themselves.

The role of marketing shifted

from pressure to permission.

The Rise of Self-Directed Buyers

The modern buyer doesn't arrive uninformed.

By the time they engage a brand, they've already:

- researched alternatives

- read reviews

- watched walkthroughs

- checked forums

- compared pricing

- evaluated credibility

Sales conversations now happen later in the journey and only if trust already exists.

This means:

- websites matter more than sales decks
- content matters more than ads
- education matters more than persuasion

The buyer journey is no longer linear.

It's investigative.

Brands that respect this autonomy win.

Brands that interrupt it lose.

Emotional Buying Didn't Disappear; It Deepened

Emotion still drives decisions. But the emotions changed.

Fear of missing out gave way to fear of regret. Excitement gave way to caution.

Status gave way to alignment.

People aren't buying to look impressive. They're buying to feel secure, confident, and understood.

The dominant emotional drivers of 2025:

- relief
- clarity
- reassurance
- belonging
- stability

The brands that speak to these emotions, not hype, build loyalty.

The Proof Economy Took Over

Claims don't convert anymore. Evidence does.

Buyers want to see:

- real outcomes
- case studies
- testimonials with specificity
- transparent pricing
- clear processes
- visible track records

Vague promises create resistance. Specific proof creates confidence.

The shift is simple:

From "trust us" to "see for yourself."

Brands that document their work outperform those that describe it.

Skepticism Became a Default Setting

The internet trained people to doubt.

Fake reviews. Sponsored opinions. Influencer fatigue. AI-generated content. Exaggerated claims. Too many burned promises.

JOIN
Achieve Systems

BECOME AN ACHIEVE SYSTEMS MEMBER TODAY!

Education
We help you get the tools to create a thriving business! It's turnkey, you can start NOW!

Marketing
We provide marketing guidelines but also plug you into our conferences, events and database

Community
We have a thriving community of entrepreneurs and business owners for you to collaborate, refer and partner with to grow and up-level your business!

WE WORK WITH ENTREPRENEURS, BUSINESS OWNERS, SPEAKERS & LEADERS!

CONTACT US OR REGISTER HERE: www.AchieveSystemsPro.com

Buyers now approach offers with skepticism by default.

This doesn't mean they're cynical. It means they're experienced.

Trust must be earned not assumed. And every inconsistency costs more than it used to.

Price Sensitivity Got Smarter

Price sensitivity isn't about being cheap.

It's about being justified. Buyers are willing to pay more but only when value is clear.

They ask:

- What am I really getting?

- What problem does this solve?

- How long will it last?

- What happens after the purchase?

Discounts without context feel suspicious.

Premium pricing without proof feels arrogant.

The winning strategy is value clarity, not price manipulation.

The Shift from Ownership to Outcomes

Buyers are less interested in owning things and more interested in results.

This is why:

- subscriptions outperform one-time purchases

- services outperform products

- education outperforms features

- access outperforms assets

People don't want stuff. They want outcomes with minimal friction.

The brands winning in 2025 sell transformation, not transactions.

Buying Became Identity-Aligned

Purchases became statements, not of status, but of values.

Buyers increasingly choose brands that:

- reflect their ethics

- align with their worldview

- respect their intelligence

- honor their time

They aren't just asking, "Does this work?"

They're asking, "Is this who I want to support?"

Identity-aligned buying isn't emotional manipulation. It's values-based decision-making.

And it's incredibly powerful.

The Decline of Hard Selling

Hard selling didn't just become ineffective; it became counterproductive.

Aggressive tactics signal desperation. Desperation signals risk.

Modern buyers respond to:

- calm confidence

- clear boundaries

- honest limitations

- transparent trade-offs

Brands that say "this isn't for everyone" build more trust than those that say "this is perfect for you."

Exclusivity today is about alignment not pressure.

Why Simplicity Converts Better Than Sophistication

Complex messaging creates friction.

The modern buyer values:

- simple explanations

- clear next steps

- predictable outcomes

- minimal commitment

Sophistication without clarity feels manipulative.

The best brands in 2025 mastered the art of making complex value feel simple, without dumbing it down.

Clarity isn't oversimplification. It's respect.

The Role of Community in Buying Decisions

People trust people more than brands.

Community validation now plays a central role in buying behavior:

- user forums

- private groups

- peer recommendations

- social proof from similar buyers

Brands that cultivate communities reduce friction across the entire decision journey.

Buying becomes less risky when others have gone first.

The New Buyer Journey Is Circular

The old funnel model assumed linear progression:

Awareness → Consideration → Purchase.

That model no longer holds.

The modern journey is circular:

- discovery
- research
- pause
- comparison
- disengagement
- return
- validation
- decision

Buyers leave and come back repeatedly.

Brands that remain helpful during disengagement earn the eventual conversion.

Patience converts.

What This Means for Marketing Teams

People trust people more than brands.

- Replace urgency with clarity
- Replace persuasion with proof
- Replace volume with relevance
- Replace funnels with ecosystems
- Replace tactics with trust

Marketing is no longer about moving people faster.

It's about helping them decide confidently.

What This Means for Sales

Sales now begins where trust already exists.

The best sales teams:

- educate instead of push
- listen more than talk
- validate concerns openly
- guide decisions without forcing them

Salespeople are no longer closers.

They're decision partners.

What This Means for Entrepreneurs

If messaging creates anxiety, hides value, relies on promises, interrupts autonomy, or lacks trustworthiness, buyers pause. In a cautious market, hesitation isn't resistance; it's the default response.

The New Truth About Buying

People don't buy when they're convinced.

They buy when they feel safe.

Safety comes from:

- clarity
- trust
- alignment
- proof
- patience

The brands that understand this don't need to shout.

They don't need to rush.

They don't need to manipulate.

They create environments where the decision feels obvious.

And in 2026, obvious beats urgent every time.

The Human Tech Revolution: Why the Next Big Innovations Aren't About AI They're About Us

Technology Didn't Make Us Obsolete. It Made Us Visible.

For the last few years, the tech conversation has been dominated by one question:

What will AI replace?

Jobs. Skills. Creativity. Judgment. Even human connection.

But in 2025, a quieter, more important question emerged:

What does technology reveal about us when it gets good enough to imitate everything else?

The answer surprised a lot of people.

As machines became faster, smarter, and more capable, the most valuable traits didn't disappear. They became clearer. Empathy. Judgment. Taste. Context. Ethics. Intuition. Creativity with intention.

In other words, the next technological leap isn't artificial.

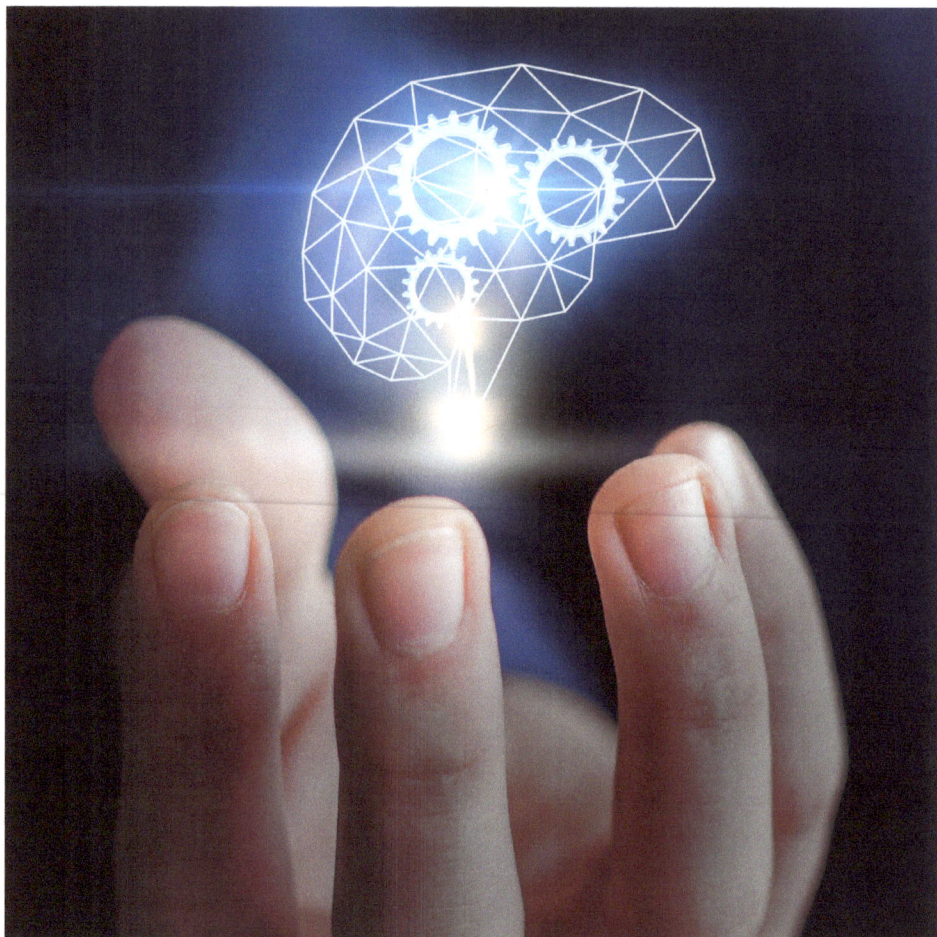

It's human.

Welcome to the Human Tech Revolution, where the most meaningful innovations aren't about replacing people, but amplifying what only people can do.

When Capability Stops Being the Differentiator

For decades, technology competed on capability. Faster processors. Bigger datasets. Better automation. More features.

AI changed that game overnight.

Suddenly, capability was abundant. Writing, designing, coding, analyzing - machines could do it all well enough. In some cases, better than humans at baseline tasks.

That abundance created a new scarcity.

When everyone can generate outputs, output stops being impressive. What matters is why something exists, how it's applied, and whether it serves real human needs.

Capability is table stakes now. Discernment is the edge.

The Shift from Automation to Augmentation

The most successful companies of 2025 didn't chase full automation. They pursued augmentation.

They asked:

- Where does AI remove friction?

- Where does human judgment still matter?

- Where does empathy outperform efficiency?

- Where does creativity require context?

The result was hybrid systems - workflows where machines handle scale and speed, while humans handle interpretation and decision-making.

This shift reframed the role of technology:

Not as a replacement for people, but as a partner.

Automation removes labor. Augmentation multiplies value.

Why "Human-Centered" Finally Became Real

Human-centered design used to be a buzzword. It sounded good in pitch decks and keynote slides, but often stopped at UX tweaks and softer language.

AI forced it to become real.

When technology began mimicking human output, companies had to confront uncomfortable truths:

- Efficiency without empathy feels cold.

- Optimization without ethics creates backlash.

- Speed without context creates harm.

The public reaction was swift. Consumers pushed back against faceless systems. Employees resisted tools that surveilled instead of supported. Regulators stepped in where companies failed to self-govern.

Human-centered tech stopped being optional.

It became a survival strategy.

MICROCASTING

Supercharge Your Business!

Do you want to find new ways to add additional income to your coaching, consulting, or content creation business?

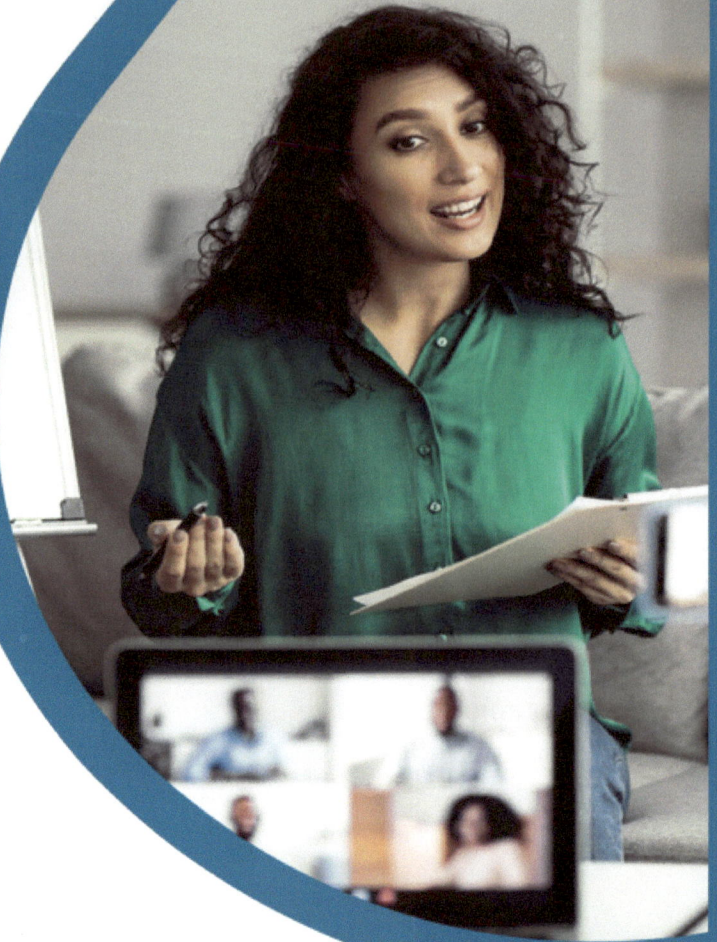

eLearning Portals by Microcasting is specifically designed for Coaches, Consultants, and Course Creators to engage your customers, establish yourself as a thought leader, and grow your revenues.

Here are just a few things you can do with **Microcasting**:

- ⊘ **Start selling** your courses and programs.
- ⊘ Create a **paid membership site** to grow your revenues.
- ⊘ Build a free membership site to **increase lead gen**.
- ⊘ Easily **integrate eLearning** into your marketing website.
- ⊘ Create **individualized customer portals** .
- ⊘ And so much more...

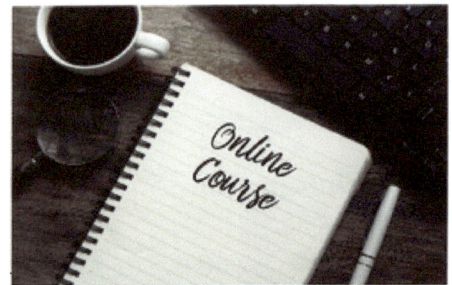

Microcasting is an all-in-one online learning platform that makes it easy for course creators to design, manage, and market their courses. With its personalized eLearning experience, you can keep your current customers engaged with your business, generating more upsells and higher renewal rates. Create courses quickly and effortlessly - all with the help of Microcasting!

Try Microcasting today and start transforming your business!

The Rise of Emotional Infrastructure

One of the most unexpected outcomes of the AI boom was the rise of emotional infrastructure - technology designed not to process data, but to support human experience.

We're seeing growth in:

- mental health platforms focused on prevention, not crisis

- workplace tools that track cognitive load, not just output

- communication systems designed to reduce mIsInterpretatIon

- wellbeing analytics integrated into performance dashboards

- digital environments that prioritize calm over stimulation

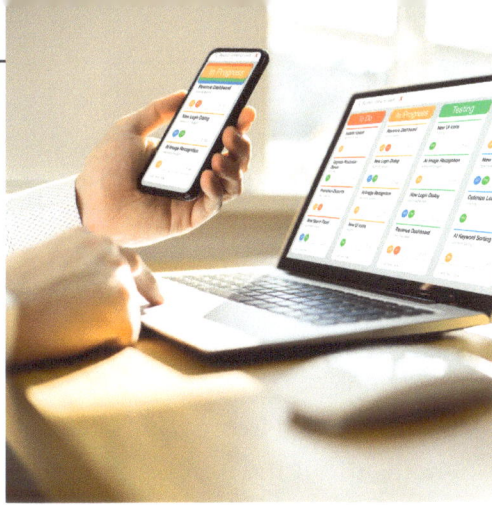

These tools don't replace human care.

They make it more accessible.

In a world optimized for speed, technology that slows people down, just enough, became revolutionary.

Trust Became a Product Feature

As technology grew more powerful, trust became more fragile.

People began asking:

- Who trained this system?

- What data does it use?

- What incentives drive its decisions?

- What happens when it gets things wrong?

Transparency turned into a competitive advantage.

The most trusted platforms of 2025 weren't the most advanced. They were the most honest. They explained limitations. Exposed trade-offs. Allowed human override.

Trust wasn't built through claims. It was built through constraints.

Technology that admitted what it couldn't do felt safer than technology that promised everything.

Taste, Judgment, and the Return of the Curator

AI is excellent at generating options.

Humans are still better at choosing between them.

This brought back the value of:

- taste

- judgment

- editorial thinking

- contextual awareness

- ethical reasoning

Curation replaced creation as the high-leverage skill.

In media, education, design, and product development, the role of the human shifted from producer to editor - shaping, refining, and contextualizing machine-generated possibilities.

The winners weren't those who generated the most.
They were those who chose the best.

Creativity Didn't Die. It Got Stricter.

There was a fear that AI would flatten creativity. Instead, it raised the bar.

When machines can generate infinite variations, originality becomes harder and more valuable.

Creative work that stood out in 2025 had:

- clear point of view
- emotional specificity
- cultural awareness
- lived experience
- intentional restraint

AI can remix and it can't care.

The human role in creativity became about meaning, not mechanics.

The Ethics Gap Became Visible

Technology always outpaces regulation. AI made that gap impossible to ignore.

Bias. Surveillance. Deepfakes. Data misuse. Decision opacity.

These weren't abstract issues. They affected real people in real ways.

Companies that ignored ethics faced backlash. Companies that embedded ethical frameworks into product design gained trust.

Ethics stopped being a legal checkbox. It became a design requirement.

The most respected tech leaders in 2025 weren't the boldest. They were the most thoughtful.

Human Skills Became Economic Assets

Soft skills stopped being soft.

Empathy. Communication. Critical thinking. Leadership.

Emotional intelligence.

These became the hardest skills to automate and the most valuable to develop.

Organizations that invested in human capability alongside technical tools outperformed those that focused only on automation.

Technology didn't eliminate the human factor.

It priced it higher.

The New Metric: Quality of Experience

Success metrics evolved.

Instead of:

- time on platform
- number of features

- automation rate

Companies measured:

- cognitive ease
- emotional friction
- trust retention
- satisfaction longevity
- user confidence

Quality of experience replaced quantity of interaction.

The best technology didn't demand attention.

It earned appreciation.

Why the Human Tech Revolution Is Just Beginning

We're still early.

Most companies are only beginning to understand what it means to design technology with people, not around them.

The next wave of innovation won't come from faster models or bigger datasets alone. It will come from better questions:

- Should this be automated?
- Who does this serve?
- What trade-offs does this introduce?
- How does this affect trust?
- What does this ask of the human on the other side?

The companies asking these questions now will define the next decade.

What This Means for Entrepreneurs

If you're building technology for 2026 and beyond, the opportunity isn't to replace humans.

It's to:

- remove friction
- amplify judgment
- support wellbeing
- enable better decisions
- respect human limits

Build tools that make people feel smarter, calmer, and more capable, not smaller, faster, and more replaceable.

The future belongs to technology that understands humans, not technology that competes with them.

The Big Shift

The first digital revolution was about access.

The second was about efficiency. The next is about human alignment.

Technology reached a point where it can do almost anything. Now it has to learn when not to. That restraint, that wisdom, will be the most powerful innovation of all.

Final Thought

The most important breakthroughs ahead won't be defined by machines becoming faster or smarter. They'll be defined by how well people are supported, empowered, and understood. Technology will fade into the background, doing its work quietly while humans gain clarity, confidence, and capacity.

Progress will show up in reduced friction, better decisions, and systems designed around real human needs rather than novelty. In that shift, innovation stops being about spectacle and starts becoming about substance. That's where the real revolution begins, not in code or hardware, but in how effectively we help people thrive.

Digital Fatigue & The Great Unplugging: Why Millions Are Choosing "Less Tech" in a More Tech World

The Problem Was Never Technology. It Was Saturation.

For years, progress was measured by connection. More devices. More platforms. More notifications. More speed.

Technology promised efficiency, freedom, and access. And for a while, it delivered. Work became flexible. Information became instant. Communities formed across borders.

But by the end of 2025, something shifted.

People weren't rejecting technology.

They were rejecting overexposure.

A quiet movement gained momentum not toward abandonment, but toward restraint. Fewer apps. Fewer alerts. Fewer platforms. More intention.

Welcome to The Great Unplugging, a cultural correction driven not by nostalgia, but by exhaustion.

Digital Fatigue Isn't Burnout. It's Overload.

Burnout implies weakness or overwork.

Digital fatigue is different.

It's the result of constant cognitive interruption.

Notifications fracture attention. Platforms compete for presence. Content never ends. Algorithms optimize for engagement, not wellbeing. The brain never signals "done."

Even when people stop scrolling, the mental residue remains.

By 2025, this state became

normalized and unsustainable.

Digital fatigue didn't arrive suddenly.

It accumulated quietly.

Why the Always-On Model Broke Down

The always-on model assumes humans can function like systems: continuously available, infinitely responsive, endlessly adaptable.

We can't.

Human cognition needs:

- pauses

- closure

- transitions

- quiet

- boredom

Technology removed those buffers.

Every spare moment became filled. Waiting disappeared. Silence vanished. Even rest became content-driven.

The result wasn't productivity. It was depletion.

The Myth of Infinite Convenience

Convenience was sold as liberation. But too much convenience removes friction that humans actually need.

Friction creates boundaries. Boundaries create recovery.

Without friction, everything bleeds together:

- work and home

- creation and consumption

- urgency and importance

The Great Unplugging isn't anti-tech. It's pro-boundary.

What the Great Unplugging Looks Like in Practice

This isn't a mass exodus from technology. It's a recalibration.

People are:

- deleting apps they don't need

- turning off non-essential

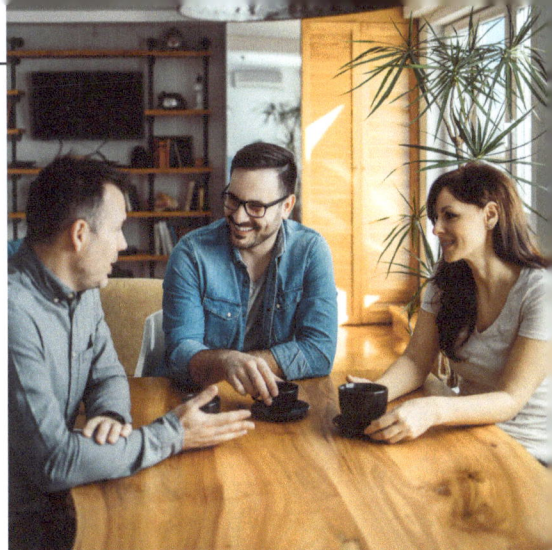

notifications

- choosing single-purpose devices

- setting screen-free hours

- moving conversations off public platforms

- prioritizing depth over reach

They're not disappearing; they're selecting.

Less noise.

More signal.

The Return of Analog Anchors

One of the clearest signs of the unplugging movement is the

resurgence of analog behaviors, not out of nostalgia, but necessity.

People are returning to:

- handwritten notes

- printed books

- in-person meetings

- physical planners

- analog hobbies

- long walks without devices

These practices provide something digital environments struggle to offer: closure.

Analog experiences end. Digital ones rarely do.

Social Media Fatigue Reached a Tipping Point

Social platforms didn't lose relevance. They lost trust.

Endless feeds created:

- comparison fatigue

- emotional whiplash

- performative identity

- algorithmic pressure

- content homogenization

People didn't stop caring about connection.

They stopped enjoying the environment.

This is why:

- private groups outperformed public feeds

- messaging replaced posting

- smaller communities replaced mass audiences

- disappearing content felt safer than permanent timelines

The unplugging movement isn't social withdrawal.

It's context control.

Productivity Culture Fueled the Exhaustion

Digital fatigue isn't just consumer-driven. It's professional.

Knowledge workers live inside tools:

- dashboards

- inboxes

- chats

- task managers

- calendars

Each promises efficiency. Together, they fragment focus.

Productivity became performative, measured by responsiveness instead of outcomes.

The Great Unplugging shows up at work as:

- fewer meetings

- asynchronous communication

- documented decisions

- deeper focus blocks

- intentional offline time

This isn't laziness. It's sustainability.

The Economics of Attention Are Being Rejected

For decades, attention noticed, monetized, and sold.

Platforms optimized for:

- time spent

- engagement loops

- emotional triggers

Users optimized for:

- relevance

- visibility

- reach

Both sides lost.

The Great Unplugging is a refusal to participate in extractive attention economics.

People are choosing tools that:

- respect time

- minimize manipulation

- prioritize usefulness over engagement

The market is responding.

Why "Less Tech" Doesn't Mean Less Progress

The assumption that progress requires maximum tech exposure is flawed.

Progress requires:

- clarity

- creativity

- energy

- focus

All of which degrade under constant digital pressure.

By unplugging strategically, people aren't falling behind. They're reclaiming capacity.

Less tech often produces better outcomes, not fewer.

Businesses Are Following the Shift

Forward-thinking companies are adapting.

They're:

- designing calmer interfaces

- reducing notification noise

- limiting features

- promoting digital wellbeing

- measuring satisfaction, not addiction

The most trusted brands of 2025 didn't try to capture more attention. They tried to deserve it.

The Mental Health Signal Companies Can't Ignore

Digital fatigue intersects directly with mental health.

Anxiety, distraction, emotional numbness, and cognitive overload avoid clinical labels but impact performance deeply.

The Great Unplugging isn't therapy.

It's prevention.

Companies ignoring this signal will face:

- disengagement

- burnout

- attrition

- declining creativity

Those that respond thoughtfully gain loyalty.

The New Digital Literacy

Digital literacy used to mean knowing how to use tools. Now it means knowing when not to.

The most capable professionals of 2025 are not the most connected.

They are the most intentional.

They choose:

- which platforms matter

- which messages deserve response

- which inputs deserve attention

This is a skill not avoidance.

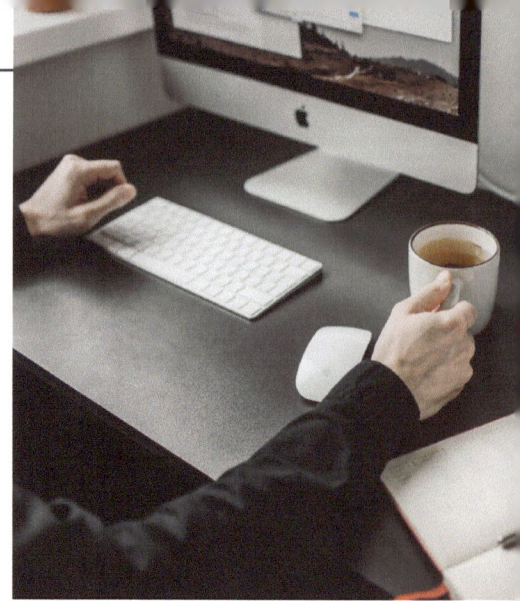

The Rise of Intentional Tech Design

The unplugging movement is influencing product design.

We're seeing:

- fewer features, better usability

- quiet modes as defaults

- humane notification systems

- clear end points in apps

- transparency around engagement mechanics

Technology is beginning to acknowledge human limits. That acknowledgment is progress.

What This Means for Leaders

Leaders set digital tone.

If leaders:

- message constantly
- expect instant replies
- reward availability
- glorify hustle

Fatigue spreads.

If leaders:

- respect boundaries
- communicate clearly
- normalize offline time
- model restraint

Recovery becomes cultural.

The Great Unplugging starts at the top.

What This Means for Creators and Brands

Attention is no longer free.

Audiences reward:

- restraint
- relevance
- respect
- usefulness

Posting less, but better, outperforms constant output. The era of saturation content is ending.

The Great Unplugging Is Not a Rejection

This is important: People are not rejecting technology. They are rejecting abuse of it.

They still want connection, innovation, and tools that help.

They just want those tools to serve human lives and not dominate them.

The Cultural Correction Is Permanent

Once people experience clarity, they don't rush back to noise.

The Great Unplugging isn't a phase.

It's a reset.

Just like:

- remote work redefined location
- slow work redefined productivity

Digital restraint is redefining progress.

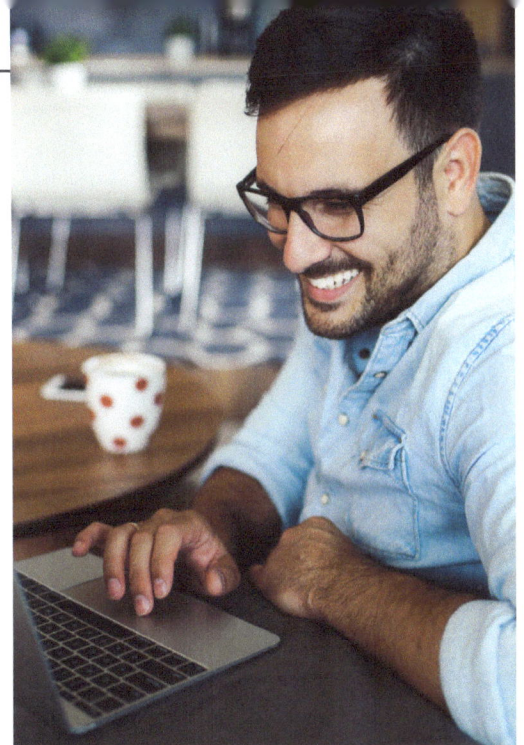

Final Thought

The future isn't unplugged. It's well-plugged. It's shaped by technology that respects human limits instead of exploiting them.

Platforms that honor attention rather than constantly compete for it. Work designed to allow recovery, reflection, and sustainable performance.

Lives built with space to breathe, not constant urgency.

In a world that has reached digital saturation, choosing less isn't a retreat or a signal of falling behind.

It's a deliberate decision to move forward with clarity and intention.

The next evolution isn't more tools or more noise. It's better alignment between technology, time, and human wellbeing.

FOR EVERY BUSINESS & BUDGET

Looking for a website design firm or D.I.Y. platform that can help you build a visually stunning and effective online brand? Look no further than our expert team. At Proshark, we help you build a customized website that meets your unique needs and goals and converts visitors to customers.

PROSHARK SITES

INNOVATION DESIGNED TO INSPIRE

www.proshark.com

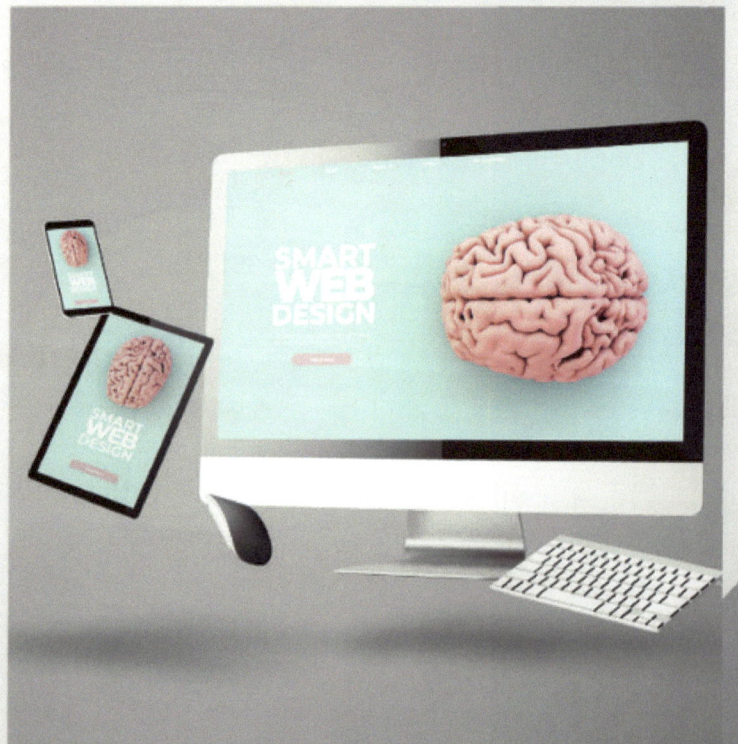

The End of Influence as We Know It: What Replaces Celebrity Culture in 2026

Fame Isn't Failing. It's Fracturing.

For most of the digital era, influence followed a simple formula: build a massive audience, maintain visibility, monetize attention.

Celebrity culture scaled online. Influencers became brands. Algorithms rewarded reach. And the loudest voices dominated the conversation.

But by the end of 2025, the system started breaking down.

Engagement fell. Trust eroded. Audiences grew skeptical. And influence, once defined by follower counts, lost its persuasive power.

This wasn't a collapse. It was a redistribution.

Influence didn't disappear. It changed shape.

Why Celebrity Influence Lost Its Grip

The old influence model relied on distance. Celebrities and top creators felt aspirational precisely because they were unreachable.

Social media erased that distance.

When everyone became accessible, constantly visible, and endlessly posting, mystique vanished. Audiences saw the mechanics behind the curtain: sponsorships, scripts, brand deals, recycled trends.

Influence became transactional.

And transactions don't inspire loyalty.

The Trust Deficit That Followed

As influencer marketing matured, so did audience skepticism.

People noticed:

- identical endorsements across creators
- vague claims without proof
- constant selling disguised as authenticity
- performative vulnerability
- opinions that shifted with sponsors

Trust cracked.

Audiences didn't reject influence.

They rejected manufactured authority.

The result was a trust deficit no amount of reach could repair.

Algorithms Accelerated the Decline

Platforms optimized for engagement, not credibility.

This rewarded:

- outrage over insight
- speed over accuracy
- repetition over originality
- volume over value

Influence became noisy.

And when everything feels amplified, nothing feels meaningful. The algorithm didn't kill influence but it exposed its fragility.

Influence Fragmented Into Communities

As mass influence weakened, micro-influence strengthened. People stopped following personalities.

They started joining communities.

Instead of asking, "Who has the biggest platform?" people asked:

- Who understands my problem?
- Who has lived this experience?
- Who has proven results?
- Who speaks my language?

Influence shifted from broadcast to belonging.

Small, trusted voices began outperforming massive ones, not

in reach, but in impact.

Credibility Replaced Charisma

Charisma once drove influence. Now credibility does.

The most influential figures entering 2026 are not celebrities. They are:

- operators
- practitioners
- educators
- builders
- specialists

They don't post constantly. They show receipts.

Their authority comes from:

- experience

- outcomes

- consistency

- clarity

They don't entertain. They inform.

And in a fatigued culture, information with integrity is magnetic.

The Rise of Contextual Influence

Influence is becoming contextual rather than universal.

Someone can be deeply influential in one niche and irrelevant elsewhere and that's the point.

Influence now depends on:

- relevance

- proximity to the problem

- shared language

- trust density

This shift rewards depth over breadth.

Influencers don't need millions of followers.

They need the right hundred.

Why Expertise Outperformed Fame

Expertise scales quietly.

Unlike fame, expertise:

- compounds

- deepens with time

- survives platform shifts

- earns respect across cycles

When audiences seek answers, not entertainment, they turn to experts.

This is why:

- long-form content resurged

- podcasts outperformed clips

- newsletters built loyal audiences

- educators replaced entertainers

Influence matured from spectacle to substance.

The Decline of the "Main Character" Economy

Influencer culture thrived on main-character energy. Every

post centered the creator. Every narrative reinforced identity as brand.

But constant self-focus fatigued audiences.

People didn't want heroes.

They wanted helpers. Influence in 2026 is shifting toward:

- facilitation

- explanation

- translation

- guidance

The most respected voices are those who elevate others not themselves.

Brands Followed the Shift

Brands noticed the change quickly.

Big influencer campaigns delivered diminishing returns. Micro-partnerships delivered trust.

Instead of paying for reach, brands began investing in:

- long-term collaborations

- expert endorsements

- community sponsorships

- practitioner advocates

Influence became relational, not transactional.

The ROI wasn't virality. It was credibility.

Why Influence Became Slower and Stronger

Old influence models optimized for speed.

New influence models optimize for durability.

Trust takes time.

Credibility requires consistency.

Reputation compounds slowly. But when influence sticks, it lasts.

A trusted voice doesn't need to shout.

Their audience listens.

The New Influence Ladder

In the emerging model, influence builds through stages:

- Competence - Can you do the thing?

- Clarity - Can you explain it well?

- Consistency - Do your actions align?

- Contribution - Do you help others succeed?

- Community - Do people gather around your work?

Fame skips steps. Real influence doesn't.

What Platforms Are Doing About It

Platforms are adapting slowly.

We're seeing:

- emphasis on meaningful interaction

- reduced emphasis on follower counts

- greater visibility for niche content

- algorithmic rewards for retention over reach

Influence is being redefined structurally.

Why This Shift Is Permanent

Celebrity culture won't disappear but it won't dominate.

The trust deficit is too deep. The audience is too aware. The market is too saturated.

Once people experience influence rooted in credibility, they don't go back.

What This Means for Entrepreneurs

If you're building influence in 2026, the playbook is clear:

- Stop chasing reach.

- Start earning trust.

- Share what works.

- Show your process.

- Serve a specific community.

- Let reputation lead.

Influence isn't about being known by everyone.

It's about being trusted by the right people.

The New Definition of Influence

Influence used to mean visibility.

Now it means impact.

It's measured by:

Influence used to mean visibility.

Now it means impact.

It's measured by:

- decisions changed

- confidence built

- problems solved

- communities strengthened

Influence no longer belongs to celebrities.

It belongs to contributors.

Final Thought

The end of influence as we knew it isn't a loss. It's a liberation. A release from constant performance, relentless pressure, and the exhausting need to pretend. The era of polished personas and manufactured relevance is losing its grip, making room for something more grounded and sustainable.

What replaces celebrity culture isn't smaller influence - it's truer influence. Influence rooted in trust, lived experience, and real contribution. It's quieter, slower, and far more resilient than viral fame. This form of influence doesn't demand perfection or spectacle. It rewards consistency, honesty, and depth over time.

Most importantly, truer influence isn't dependent on algorithms or fleeting trends. It doesn't vanish when platforms shift or reach fluctuates. It endures because it's built on human connection, not digital validation. And in that endurance lies its real power.

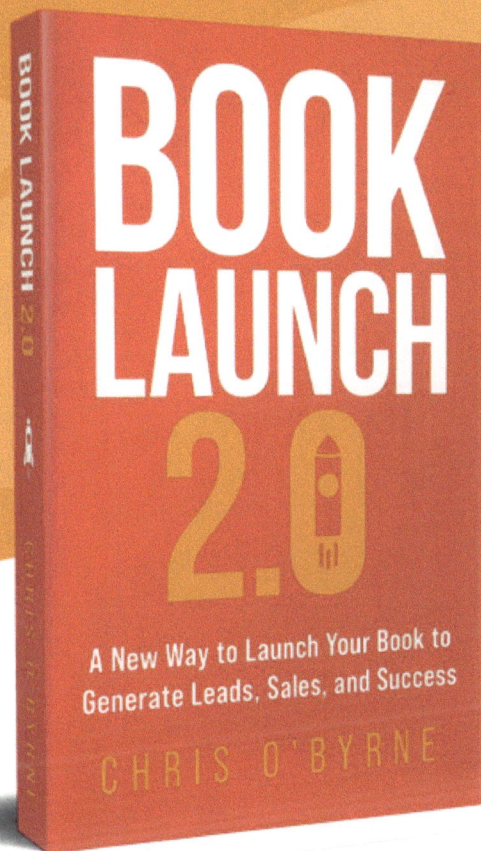

FROGMAN MINDFULNESS

Jon Macaskill
US Navy SEAL Commander (Ret)
Keynote Speaking
One on One Coaching
Mindfulness Teaching
www.frogmanmindfulness.com
757-619-1211